Assertiveness

Leeds Metropolitan University

D0265427

About the series

Your Personal Trainer is a series of five books designed to help you learn, or develop, key business skills. Fun, flexible and involving (and written by experienced, real-life trainers), each title in the series acts as your very own 'personal fitness trainer', allowing you to focus on your own individual experience and identify priorities for action.

Assertiveness   1 904298 13 3
Stress Management 1 904298 17 6
Interviewing Skills   1 904298 14 1
Negotiating Skills   1 904298 15 X
Time Management   1 904298 16 8

Assertiveness

by Jeanie Civil

First published in 2003 by
Spiro Press
17–19 Rochester Row
London SW1P 1LA
Telephone: +44 (0)870 400 1000

© Jeanie Civil, 2003

© Typographical arrangement, Spiro Press, 2003

ISBN 1 904298 13 3

British Library Cataloguing-in-Publication Data.
A catalogue record for this book is available from the British Library.

Library of Congress Cataloging-in-Publication. Data on file.

All rights reserved. No part of this publication may be reproduced,
stored in a retrieval system or transmitted, in any form or by any
means, electronic, mechanical, photocopying, recording and/or
otherwise, without the prior written permission of the publishers.
This may not be lent, resold, hired out or otherwise disposed of by
way of trade in any form, binding or cover other than that in
which it is published without the prior written permission of the
publishers.

Jeanie Civil asserts her moral right to be identified as the author
of this work.

Series devised by: Astrid French and Susannah Lear
Series Editor: Astrid French

Spiro Press USA
3 Front Street
Suite 331
PO Box 338
Rollinsford NH 03869
USA

LEEDS METROPOLITAN
UNIVERSITY
LEARNING CENTRE

1704069579
CALL
GEN-53716
19·8·04
650.13 CIV

Typeset by: Q3 Digital/Litho, Queens Road, Loughborough
Printed in Great Britain by: Cromwell Press
Cover image by: PhotoDisc
Cover design by: Cachet Creatives

To Eva and Jack Barnes,
my assertive role models

Contents

Introduction

Welcome to *Assertiveness*, part of a brand new series – **Your Personal Trainer** – which offers you an exciting new way to learn, or develop, key business skills. Fun, flexible and involving, each title in this series acts as your very own 'personal fitness trainer', allowing you to focus on your individual experience and identify priorities for action. Designed as a self-development workbook, each title creates an individual record of what you have achieved.

This book focuses on developing your *assertiveness*, a key skill for success at both work and home. It gives you the opportunity of assessing where you are now, and opens doors for where you might like to be, or go, in the future. It will help you find new and more appropriate ways of relating to people and situations.

> *WATCH OUT FOR YOUR TRAINER*
> He will give you tips and alert you to potential areas of concern as you work your way through the book.

Everyone is capable of becoming more assertive – though there will be challenges to meet along the way. Becoming 'fit' in assertiveness is as much about confidence and self-esteem as it is about techniques. The ideas and exercises in this book may be a little uncomfortable at first. However, by keeping an open mind and putting in some practice, assertiveness can become part of your everyday responses and help you gain confidence in achieving results that satisfy both you and others.

To be described as assertive may not always feel like a compliment... This could be because so many people confuse assertiveness with aggressiveness. Hence 'She's very assertive in meetings' can sound like 'She takes over' or 'She's bossy'. Similarly, 'He was very assertive when he said the project was his responsibility not mine' can be perceived as 'He's aggressive' or 'He's a bully'. Not so! If you are assertive then none of these adjectives applies. What, then, is assertiveness?

What is assertiveness?

Assertiveness is about being open, honest and direct. It is about being focused and asking for what you want or need – while recognizing that others also have needs. It is *not* to be confused with aggressive or appeasing behaviour (non-assertive behaviour), but more about this later.

It is easy to be assertive when you are feeling positive, but almost everybody will sometimes feel negative about his or her ability to stand up to pressure. It is on these occasions that we resort to our primitive *fight*, *flight*, *fright* or *freeze* impulse.

Feeling:

Justifiable anger towards someone may mean that you want to fight back (*fight*)

Rejected for a job may mean you just want to run away from the situation (*flight*)

Under pressure from your line manager may mean that you behave in a frightened way (*fright*)

Threatened by a bully may result in you being unable to respond (*freeze*).

Assertiveness will help you develop more positive strategies.

So, what do you gain, or lose, by being assertive?

You gain:

✔ self-love and improved self-worth
✔ self-confidence
✔ improved quality of life
✔ trust
✔ respect
✔ influence
✔ genuine relationships.

You lose:

✘ nothing.

And what do you gain, or lose, by being non-assertive?

You gain:

- ✔ a quiet life
- ✔ avoidance of conflict
- ✔ control of inner feelings
- ✔ praise for conforming
- ✔ feelings that you are being used
- ✔ sometimes depression and psychosomatic illness.

You lose:

- ✘ the ability to clear the atmosphere of conflict
- ✘ the respect of others
- ✘ the power to make decisions
- ✘ success in relationships
- ✘ psychosomatic well-being.

So, ask yourself the question; are you happy with your gains, or are the losses in your life greater? Would you give up some of the gains of being non-assertive for the positive aspects of being mentally happier and healthier?

If so, read on…

This is a book for anyone who wants to learn the physical, psychological and behavioural skills of becoming assertive, and have some fun while doing so! Whether developing your assertiveness skills from scratch, or brushing up on what you already know, enjoy your read, and enjoy the benefits of becoming a more assertive person.

How to use this book

This book has been produced in a flexible format so you can maximize your individual potential for learning. You will have to put some work into it, but you should have some fun along the way.

The book is divided into four main parts:
Fitness Assessment
Fitness Profile
Work-out
Keeping Fit.

Fitness Assessment consists of 10 individual assessments. These assessments are grouped into four key skills areas or sections:

Self-confidence
Getting things done
Managing conflict, and
Values and rights.

The assessments offer a range of questions, exercises, choices of behaviour and attitudes to test your current skills fitness.

Try and be as honest and objective as possible when completing this part so that you have a realistic idea of your current 'fitness' in assertiveness. And remember, there are no right or wrong answers, only feedback!

Fitness Profile gives you the results of your Fitness Assessment. It helps you to understand your responses and identify both personal strengths and weaknesses/areas for development.

Work-out offers a range of practical activities and exercises to improve your skills and help you become 'super-fit' at assertiveness.

Keeping Fit reminds you of the importance of practising

your skills and allows you to develop a personal fitness plan.

You will get the most out of this book if you work through it systematically, checking up on your assertiveness skills from 1-10. This will enable you to get a good overall view of your fitness.

However, you may choose to focus on a particular area of the skill (eg Managing conflict), working through the relevant section in Fitness Assessment then moving on to subsequent sections in Fitness Profile and Work-out. These sections are clearly marked in the text, with directions to follow-up reading *at the end of each section.*

Finally, if you want a quick review of key learning points, check out the summary checklists at the end of each section in Work-out.

Whichever way you choose to use this book, enjoy the experience!

Fitness Assessment

Fitness Assessment

Fitness Assessment has been designed to test your current skills fitness.

If you want an overall picture of your skills fitness (which is recommended) you need to work through all 10 assessments and then move on to subsequent parts – Fitness Profile, Workout and Keeping Fit.

*If, however, you don't have the time to work through all the assessments, or wish to focus your learning, you can concentrate on those sections which develop a particular aspect of the skill, and then only work through relevant subsequent sections. If you do decide to do this, however, make sure that you work through **all** the assessments within the individual sections.*

Assessments 1-3 focus on your **Self-confidence**
Assessments 4-6 focus on **Getting things done**
Assessments 7-8 on **Managing conflict**
Assessments 9-10 on **Values and rights.**

So, let's test your current skills fitness.

Self-confidence

In order to be assertive you need to be able to speak and act in an open, honest and direct way. You need to be able to contribute to meetings, deal with conflict and express your values and opinions. This requires self-confidence. Assessments 1-3 focus on self-confidence. They try to help you recognize and understand how you think and feel about situations and people, and the impact this has on your behaviour. If you feel confident in yourself your behaviour will naturally be more assertive. If you lack confidence, however, you may behave less assertively.

TRAINER'S WARNING

Don't forget to answer these questions honestly; make sure you get a true picture of your fitness.

TRAINER'S TIP

Feel free to change the genders in any of the examples offered; you may find this helps you relate to the situations.

ASSESSMENT 1: ANCESTRAL VOICES

Your natural self-confidence can be affected by a number of factors – who is present, their relationship to you and, most significantly, your early childhood messages; how you were told to think, feel or behave when you were small. Although other people may also have affected your self-image – partners, associates or colleagues – these 'ancestral voices' stay with you, 'chatting' to you incessantly, like little creatures sitting on your shoulder. Unless you become aware of them these voices can seriously dent your self-confidence and encourage non-assertive behaviour.

Answer the questions overleaf to discover your ancestral voices. Tick the Yes or the No box for each question. If you are wavering then your answer is probably Yes. Commit yourself; don't leave a question unanswered.

		Yes	No
1	Are you reluctant to show your feelings?	☐	☐
2	When setting standards for yourself are they usually too high?	☐	☐
3	Do you sometimes feel 'put upon' when helping others?	☐	☐
4	Do you take on too many jobs at the same time?	☐	☐
5	Do you dislike letting go of a job, thinking 'with a bit more effort I could improve this task'?	☐	☐
6	Do you like to get things *right*?	☐	☐
7	Do you like to be liked, preferring to be popular than unpopular?	☐	☐
8	Do you find it difficult to delegate or ask for help?	☐	☐
9	Do little things annoy you; a picture not quite straight, a disorderly desk, spelling mistakes?	☐	☐
10	Do you tend to collect for somebody's present or organize your work's social gatherings?	☐	☐
11	Do you become irritated when someone takes ages to come to the point?	☐	☐
12	Do you use other people, or their work, as a yardstick for your own performance and judge yourself accordingly?	☐	☐
13	Are you reluctant to give up a job, or stop reading a book, which you are not enjoying?	☐	☐
14	Do you go to work when you are feeling ill even though others would stay away with the same symptoms?	☐	☐
15	Do you finish off, or add to, people's sentences in the hope that they'll get on with it?	☐	☐
16	Do you like to be organized and keep things neat and tidy?	☐	☐
17	Do you hate people wasting time talking about what they might do, instead of just doing it?	☐	☐

18 Would you find it difficult to share your
personal concerns with someone?   □   □
19 Do you try to avoid conflict so as not to upset
other people?   □   □
20 Do you push yourself to achieve a better job or
relationship, or to gain more qualifications? □   □

Complete the following five columns (A-E), putting your score next to the question numbers below. Give yourself 1 point if you have answered Yes, 0 points if No. Calculate your score for each column.

Column	A	B	C	D	E
Questions	2 ☐	3 ☐	4 ☐	1 ☐	5 ☐
Questions	6 ☐	7 ☐	11☐	8 ☐	12☐
Questions	9 ☐	10☐	15☐	14☐	13☐
Questions	16☐	19☐	17☐	18☐	20☐
TOTAL SCORE	☐	☐	☐	☐	☐

ASSESSMENT 2: GIVING AND RECEIVING COMPLIMENTS

Being able to give and receive compliments without embarrassment or denial reflects a healthy level of self-confidence and self-worth. How fit are you at giving and receiving compliments?

Look at the scenarios below. Tick your most likely response.

1 Your boss compliments you on a report you have prepared. What do you think, say or do?

    A   Reply 'Thanks, but I don't really think it's that
        great', or   □
    B   'Thank you, that feels good.'   □
    C   Think to yourself 'What are they after?'   □

2 David, a junior member of your team, has just delivered an excellent presentation to one of your clients. What do you think, say or do?

    A Think to yourself 'Keep your hands off, this one's mine!', or ☐

    B 'Oh well, they'll probably want David, not me, to handle their account from now on.' ☐

    C Walk over and say 'Well done, first-rate presentation. I really think it went down well.' ☐

3 You are congratulated on winning promotion. What do you think, say or do?

    A Say 'Thanks, I'm absolutely thrilled with the promotion', or ☐

    B 'I should think so too after all the hard work I have put into this company', or ☐

    C 'It is a fluke, I don't really deserve it!' ☐

ASSESSMENT 3: BODY LANGUAGE

Your body talks! How you think and feel about yourself, situations and people is reflected in your body language; and this in turn is picked up and interpreted by those around you. You need to be aware of your body language – and that of other people. After all, it's no use speaking in an assertive manner if your body language is telling another story… You need to appear confident, even though inwardly you may feel anxious or nervous.

Look at the illustrations opposite and, under each one, write down what you think the body language is 'saying' or implying. The body language may be interpreted as:

    Avoiding (withdrawn, retiring)
    Adapting (compromising)
    Appeasing (pleasing others)
    Aggressive (threatening)
    Assertive (direct, open).

TRAINER'S WARNING

People from different cultural backgrounds may interpret body language differently.

TRAINER'S WARNING

In face-to-face communication, body language accounts for some 55% of someone's impression of you, voice 38%, content only 7%.

1 [Arms behind head]

....

2 [Turned-up feet]

....

3 [Eyes lowered]

....

4 [Pointed finger]

....

5 [Hands on mouth]

....

6 [Twirling hair]

....

Ideally, you should work through all 10 assessments to get an overall view of your assertiveness fitness. If, however, you wish to focus on developing your self-confidence ➡ Self-confidence Fitness Profile p. 29.

Getting things done

Becoming assertive will help you to organize your own work and stop you becoming a dumping ground for other people's unwanted work. The direct, honest approach of assertiveness will also help you to raise the standard of work of colleagues for whom you have responsibility and make you more adept at handling difficult situations and making positive contacts and relationships. It will help you to get things done!

The following three assessments concentrate on getting things done.

ASSESSMENT 4: MEETINGS

TRAINER'S WARNING

Don't forget to answer these questions honestly – make sure you get a true picture of your fitness.

Meetings are a key forum for discussing and agreeing issues – for getting things done. In order to make the most of meetings you need to speak and act assertively, mastering key skills such as keeping the meeting to time, handling interruptions and speaking up if you don't understand something or need clarification.

TRAINER'S TIP

Feel free to change the genders in any of the examples offered; you may find that this helps you relate more effectively to the situations.

Look at the following situations. Tick your most likely response.

1　Someone arrives late for a meeting you
　　are chairing; what do you say?
　　A　'Don't worry, we've only just begun the real meat of
　　　　the meeting.'　☐
　　B　'Nice of you to turn up, eventually.'　☐
　　C　'I would appreciate you coming on time to these
　　　　meetings.'　☐

2 Someone is dominating discussions; what do you say or do?

A   Sit there and say nothing. ☐

B   Fold your arms, play with your papers and ignore them. ☐

C   Say 'I think it would be useful if you gave someone else an opportunity to air their opinions.' ☐

3 Someone is wandering off the issue being discussed, in an amusing way; what do you say or do?

A   Say 'That's really funny, however, we do need to get through this agenda by noon. Maybe you could tell these stories over lunch?' ☐

B   Say 'It's very irritating when you keep going off the point. Stick to the agenda.' ☐

C   Say nothing but feel upset and annoyed. ☐

4 Someone keeps interrupting in the meeting; how do you respond?

A   Sit there and say nothing. ☐

B   Say 'Please allow people to finish their point before interrupting.' ☐

C   Say 'Look, you've had your turn; try shutting up for a bit.' ☐

5 Something is being discussed that you don't understand; how do you respond?

A   Change the subject. ☐

B   Say 'I don't understand what you are saying, please will you briefly explain it to me?' ☐

C   Think to yourself 'I'm really stupid if everyone else around the table understands what is being discussed' and say nothing. ☐

LEEDS METROPOLITAN UNIVERSITY LEARNING CENTRE

6   Something is being discussed with which you do not
       agree. What do you say or do?
   A   Say nothing, as you really want this person's
       approval.   ☐
   B   Say 'That's a load of rubbish.'   ☐
   C   Say 'I agree with part of what you are saying,
       however, I need to say that I disagree with your last
       point.'   ☐

ASSESSMENT 5: SAYING NO

While you may be very effective at getting things done for
yourself, and for certain other people, you may find it difficult
to say No to certain individuals or requests. This can lead to
work overload and stop you getting things done.

   Saying No to a particular person or request can be difficult,
even for usually assertive people. Sometimes this can be due
to family values and culture which emphasize the need to put
other people first, respect your elders and betters etc.

*Look at the following list of people; to whom do you find it
difficult to say No? Tick the relevant box/boxes.*

1   To whom do you find it difficult to say No?
   A   A life partner?   ☐
   B   One of your children?   ☐
   C   A certain relative?   ☐
   D   One of your friends?   ☐
   E   A business partner?   ☐
   F   An employer?   ☐
   G   A colleague?   ☐
   H   A specific teacher?   ☐
   I   A doctor?   ☐
   J   A police officer?   ☐
   K   A sales person?   ☐
   L   Other people?   ☐
Name them..
Number of boxes ticked   SCORE

2 To which of the following do you find it difficult to say No?

   A A request to work late by your boss, even though this clashes with your plans? ☐

   B A request to give a colleague a lift, even though it's out of your way? ☐

   C A favour from your children? ☐

   D A request to lend money or an item? ☐

   E A job offer, even though you know it's not right for you? ☐

   F Other requests? ☐

Name them ....

Number of boxes ticked   SCORE

3 If someone held a contrary view to you about any of the following topics, and asked whether you agreed with their view, about which topic/s would you be able to say assertively 'No, I disagree'?

   A Sexual orientation ☐

   B Politics ☐

   C Racial equality ☐

   D Private education ☐

   E Your accomplishments ☐

   F Your mistakes ☐

   G Others' mistakes ☐

   H Abortion ☐

   I A colleague's behaviour/attitude ☐

   J Capital punishment ☐

   K Chauvinism ☐

   L Other views ☐

Name them ....

Number of boxes ticked   SCORE

Give yourself 3 marks for all the boxes ticked in question 3. Deduct 1 mark for all the boxes ticked in questions 1 and 2.

TOTAL ASSESSMENT 5 SCORE

ASSESSMENT 6: DEALING WITH MANIPULATION

When people try to manipulate you they are looking for a pay-off. This means they gain something for themselves, either a certain feeling or something they want from you. You need to be able to recognize what manipulators are trying to achieve for themselves, otherwise it prevents *you* from achieving *your* goals. Address the manipulation – openly – so that you can achieve your goals, and get things done. Handling manipulation assertively brings people together in an open, honest relationship. If you are able to do this you will not only get things done, you will also feel more personally assured.

Generally, people will try to manipulate you by working on certain 'psychological triggers' or perceived weaknesses. They may try to:

A   Work on your vulnerabilities or 'crumple button'
B   Appeal to your emotions
C   Appeal to your intellect
D   Hook your ancestral voices
E   Play on your friendship
F   Use their status
G   Appeal to your values
H   Play on your loyalty
I   Make you look foolish or put you down
J   Get what they want regardless of your needs.

Try to identify what kind of manipulation is being used in the following examples. Choose the appropriate letter from A-J, and write it in the box provided.

1   'I realize that you're keen to get away for the weekend, but could you just do this photocopying for me before you leave?'   ☐

2 'You are the best public speaker we have, so I want you, rather than me, to give this presentation to the staff.' ☐

3 'I recognize that you have to go to a funeral, however, you must be back by 4pm for this vital meeting.' ☐

4 'I know how loyal you are to me as your boss so you have to attend the residential conference regardless of the difficulties you are having with your partner.' ☐

5 'I understand how disappointed you were when you didn't get the last promotion, but this will give you the opportunity to show how the wrong person was promoted.' ☐

6 'I expect you to refer all queries and ideas to me as your line manager before discussing them at the directors' meeting.' ☐

Ideally, you should work through all 10 assessments to get an overall view of your skills fitness. If, however, you wish to focus on developing your ability to get things done ➡ Getting things done Fitness Profile p.37.

Managing conflict

However assertive you are in your day-to-day work, at home, in shops, or in your many different relationships, it can be difficult to be assertive in the face of conflict. It is in times of conflict that those primitive responses of fight, flight, fright or freeze come to the front of your feelings, your thoughts and, therefore, your behaviour.

Assertiveness will help you respond to conflict positively, and not resort to these instinctive behaviours. The following two assessments focus on managing conflict.

ASSESSMENT 7: IDENTIFYING AND MANAGING CONFLICT

Conflict can take a number of different forms:

Inner conflict (when what you have to do is different from what you want to do)

Organizational conflict (when the organizational culture and values are different from your own)

Team conflict
Conflict between two people for whom you have responsibility,

and

Conflict with one other person.

TRAINER'S WARNING
Don't select the one that you think is the 'right' or 'best' answer. Work quickly and be honest, otherwise you will only cheat yourself.

TRAINER'S TIP
Feel free to change the genders or the personnel involved in any of the examples offered. You may find this helps you relate better to the situations.

The following assessment will help you identify, and manage, different forms of conflict.

Read through the following scenarios. What form of conflict do they involve? Now tick your most likely response to these scenarios.

1   You are experiencing personal, family or relationship problems; you need to take some time off work. How do you respond?
    A   Say nothing.   ☐
    B   Talk with someone you like to gain reassurance that it is not your fault.   ☐
    C   Tell half-truths: consider taking sick leave.   ☐
    D   Stay at work and involve yourself in frantic activity.   ☐
    E   Discuss with your line manager that you are having some personal difficulties and that it may be necessary to have some time away from work, which you will make up.   ☐

2 You are receiving complaints from several members of your staff about the slackness of one of the team. What do you do or say?

A Say nothing. ☐

B Smile at the team member concerned when you see them. ☐

C Suggest that the rest of the team do a little extra work to cover. ☐

D See the person concerned and tell them to perform to standard, otherwise face the discipline procedure. ☐

E Call the team together and ask them to voice their concerns about the 'team dynamics'. ☐

3 You have to make five redundancies. How do you respond?

A Do nothing; things might change. ☐

B Worry about each person; consider their home life and how they will suffer. ☐

C Decide which five you want to go, based upon your redundancy policy, but don't take any action. ☐

D Talk to all staff about the redundancies. Ask for volunteers first and then draw up a 'possibles' list, following consultation with staff and in the light of company regulations. ☐

E Suggest to your line manager that you could make some people part-time. ☐

4 Two of your staff have conflict between them. They each come separately to you and complain about the other. How do you deal with the problem?

A Bring the two of them together and ask them to tell each other what the issues are, and how they can be resolved. ☐

B   Agree with each person that it must be difficult. Say that you are glad that they feel they can come and talk to you, but do nothing.   ☐

C   Suggest that they do the jobs they think they can manage to do without much difficulty and forget the area of conflict.   ☐

D   Say that you are not there to sort out relationships; you have more important targets to achieve.   ☐

E   Take no notice.   ☐

5   You are experiencing unjust treatment, bullying or harassment from someone at work. How do you respond?

A   Avoid the person.   ☐

B   Talk to the person concerned about the behaviour that you have observed, tell them how you feel and say what you need, in terms of their treatment of you.   ☐

C   Think 'Well, they can be all right some of the time so that should be enough.'   ☐

D   Tell their line manager and suggest that the person concerned should leave.   ☐

E   Try to be nice to them. Exchange pleasantries each time you see them.   ☐

ASSESSMENT 8: GIVING AND RECEIVING CRITICISM

Practically everyone is criticized from time to time – sometimes with good reason, sometimes not; sometimes constructively, sometimes not. From time to time, also, we all feel the need to criticize others. Giving criticism can be as daunting as receiving it; get it wrong and you can make a situation worse.

Look at the following situations. How would you respond? Circle 1, 2 or 3 as shown in the key opposite.

KEY
1   I am least likely to respond in this way
2   I might respond in this way; the other two options don't appeal
3   I am most likely to respond in this way

1   For the first time in months you are late for a one-to-one meeting. Your colleague exclaims 'You are always late for my meetings!' How do you respond?
A Walk away and get angry.	1	2	3
B Justify your behaviour.	1	2	3
C Ask for specific examples.	1	2	3

2   You are being reprimanded in front of your colleagues. How do you respond?
A Say 'I think it is inappropriate to discuss this with other people present.'	1	2	3
B Cry.	1	2	3
C Blame other colleagues or circumstances.	1	2	3

3   Your manager has recently cancelled two meetings with you at short notice. You are annoyed and complain to a director. Your manager is then upset to receive feedback from a director rather than you first; she questions your behaviour. How do you react?
A Say 'Well, you are never here.'	1	2	3
B Say 'I'm sorry, you are right. It won't happen again.'	1	2	3
C Say nothing, and then moan to your colleagues about what a rotten manager he or she is.	1	2	3

4   Some of your colleagues are feeling demotivated; you need to pass on some critical feedback to your manager. What do you say?

A 'Two members of the team are feeling very demotivated, mainly because you hardly ever praise them for the extra work they do for you in their own time.'   1   2   3
B 'Everyone in the team is demotivated.'
                                        1   2   3
C 'Everyone thinks that you're a useless manager.'
                                        1   2   3

Ideally, you should work through all 10 assessments to get a good overall view of your skills fitness. If, however, you wish to focus on your ability to manage conflict ➡ Managing conflict Fitness Profile p.44.

TRAINER'S WARNING

Don't forget to answer these questions honestly; make sure that you get a true picture of your fitness.

Values and rights

In order to be assertive you need to understand your rights and know when and how to establish your values. This requires courage and a belief that you have the right to hold a different opinion to the one being given. The following two assessments focus on your values and rights.

TRAINER'S TIP

Feel free to change the genders in any of the examples offered. You may find this helps you relate to the situations.

ASSESSMENT 9: ESTABLISHING YOUR VALUES

People you like usually share your values and belief systems (on politics, religion, race, sex, sexuality). You probably find them easier to get on with since you 'talk the same language' and are starting from the same point of view. You are likely to be assertive with such people. Conversely, you tend to be less assertive with people you don't like. You may dislike them with good reason (perhaps they hold racist or sexist views), but beware of not liking people for the wrong reasons; maybe they got a job you applied for; maybe you feel insecure about your abilities and resent their skills; maybe they simply have the wrong accent or you don't like their dress sense!

Look at the following situations. Do you believe you could establish your values in these circumstances? How would you think, feel or behave?

1   You are on a selection panel for a new post. One of the candidates is black. This person is your first choice. In the post-interview discussions you hear general disquiet about his race. Telephone checks are made until some incident or reason is found to justify his non appointment. Would you:

   A   Say something immediately about what you are picking up as prejudicial comments? ☐

   B   Report it? ☐

   C   Feel upset but say nothing? ☐

   D   Comment on the fact that not every candidate was checked in this way and that if a search were made on anyone some negative comment was bound to surface? ☐

2   A senior colleague is talking to you about a homosexual that you both know and work with. Your colleague remarks 'I don't mind what they do in private, but kissing in public is disgusting. I'd give them what for if they approached me!' Would you:

   A   Ask if they object to heterosexuals kissing in public? ☐

   B   Say nothing? ☐

   C   Address their anxiety about sexual orientation? ☐

   D   Say 'Research suggests that when people are homophobic it is because they don't want to address their own homosexuality'? ☐

3 You (a woman) are being informally interviewed for a job. You are casually asked a question about your plans for having a family. How would you respond?

A Say 'That seems like a sexist comment to me!' ☐

B Say 'Have you asked all of the candidates the same question?' ☐

C Report the incident. ☐

D Smile and say 'I don't know yet.' ☐

4 You are invited to a mixed religion wedding. One of the guests comments on how the marriage is doomed to fail because the couple are from different religions and cultures. Would you:

A Think 'I can't be bothered arguing'? ☐

B Feel unsettled but say nothing? ☐

C Say that you disagree? ☐

D Say 'I believe that it is the way each person treats one another as an emotional human being that makes or breaks a marriage. It is not automatically about their religious beliefs'? ☐

ASSESSMENT 10: RIGHTS

TRAINER'S WARNING

Bear in mind that you need to exercise these rights within the rights/laws of different cultures and countries.

How good are you at standing up for your rights? *You do have certain rights.* Lawyers may disagree with this wording, but for the purposes of this book consider your rights from a *moral* rather than a strict legal perspective.

Below is a list of statements. Tick those with which you readily agree.

You have the right to have rights ☐

You have the right to assert yourself ☐

You have the right to feel ☐

You have the right to make mistakes ☐

You have the right to be protected by the law ☐

You have the right to free speech (but be aware of the
effect of your words on other people) ☐

You have the right to feel secure ☐

You have the right to be happy ☐

You have the right to be ill ☐

You have the right to be treated with respect ☐

You have the right to grieve ☐

You have the right to give others their rights ☐

You have the right to ask for more time to respond ☐

You have the right to do nothing or be non-assertive ☐

You have the right to say something is 'good enough' ☐

You have the right to enjoy your sexuality ☐

You have the right not to be overlooked ☐

You have the right not to be physically or emotionally
abused ☐

SCORE

Total number of ticks

Make a brief note of the statements you didn't tick.

....
....
....
....
....
....

Now, next to these statements, write down how they make
you feel – angry, frightened, embarrassed, passionate,
uncomfortable?

Ideally, you will now have completed all 10 assessments
and have a good overall view of your skills fitness. If so ➡
Fitness Profile p.25.

If, however, you have chosen to focus on your values and
rights ➡ Values and rights Fitness Profile p.48.

Fitness Profile

Fitness Profile

Well done, you've completed Fitness Assessment – now you can find out the results!

Fitness Profile allows you to evaluate your current skills fitness – your strengths, weaknesses and priorities for action. It builds up into a fitness profile unique to you. Fitness profiles 1-3 relate directly to assessments 1-3. Similarly, profiles 4-6, 7-8 and 9-10.

Self-confidence

The following three profiles will help you build up a picture of how self-confident you are, a key element of assertiveness.

PROFILE 1: ANCESTRAL VOICES

We have discussed the idea of 'creatures' sitting on your shoulder giving you messages about how you should think or behave. These creatures were put on your shoulder when you were young. Whether your childhood experiences were essentially positive or negative, you were still given early behavioural messages – what and how to eat, what to wear etc. Some of these messages may have been positive and helpful like 'be happy', but others may have been unhelpful such as you're 'no good at sports', 'a nasty, horrid person' or 'not as talented as your sister/brother' and had long-term negative effects. As you have matured, some of these 'creatures' may have dropped off your shoulder; nonetheless, let's have a look to see if some are still hanging around.

Look back to assessment 1 (p.7) and make a note of your individual column scores below.

Column	A	B	C	D	E
	☐	☐	☐	☐	☐

> For this assessment, if you have a score of 3 or more in any one column you probably display a particular kind of behaviour. What do the columns tell you?

Column A – The 'Be Perfect' person
Column B – The 'Pleasing People' person
Column C – The 'Hurry Up' person
Column D – The 'Be Strong' person
Column E – The 'Try Harder' person

THE BE PERFECT PERSON

Imagine the Be Perfect person lives in a room full of diamonds; diamond ceiling, floor and walls. Yet right in the corner is a load of manure. Instead of seeing the diamonds, the Be Perfect person focuses on the manure. Similarly, they tend to focus on what is *wrong* with someone rather than what is right. If you are a Be Perfect person you may play the psychological game of 'blemish', which is looking for the mistake rather than appreciating the whole. For example, someone hands you a finished project and your first reaction is 'There's a spelling mistake on page 90' instead of saying 'Thank you, there's a lot of good work gone into this. However, I am concerned about one or two spelling mistakes, let's get those right.'

As a child you were probably told to aim for perfection. Scripts like 'If a job's worth doing it's worth doing well'. So you tend to work at 100% all the time, rather than at 80%, which is achievable. Nobody is capable of working 100% all the time.

THE PLEASING PEOPLE PERSON

If you have found this creature chatting to you, then you will probably nod a lot and smile, even when you don't agree with someone or feel upset! You are probably liked but may come across as ineffectual when it comes to sorting out conflict.

When you were small you were probably told 'Think about what the neighbours will say' or 'Be nice to people'. The message that you were picking up is that unless you are pleasant to people you are no good. Somehow you will be punished. So your style is to make others feel good so you can feel better. You find it really difficult to say No.

THE HURRY UP PERSON

Gosh, everything is such a rush for you. You are always busy doing so many things simultaneously. Hurrying here hurrying there but still thinking about what else you ought to be doing instead. When you are in a meeting you think about whom you need to speak to at lunch. When you are at lunch you are thinking about being back in the meeting. You probably tap your fingers or twitch your leg more than most. Your speed is admirable, but how are the people around you affected? They try to stop you in the corridor but you are in a hurry; 'I'll see you later' you reply, but 'later' you're still just as busy. You probably arrive late for meetings, letting everyone know how busy you've been. You can irritate others with your inability to listen and reflect.

As a child you were probably told to hurry up. 'We haven't got time to stand and wait, get on with it'; 'Hurry up, we need to be at your grandpa's in ten minutes. Be quick.' This message may have stuck; though, probably, it's no longer appropriate.

THE BE STRONG PERSON

You hardly ever have time off work and go in even when you are ill and others are off sick with the same condition. Not you; you're there rain or shine, in sickness and in health, never recognizing when you're tired or hungry, keeping going. You wait until the weekend or holidays to be ill.

When you were small you were probably told to be strong and keep your feelings to yourself. Sayings like 'Big boys don't cry'; 'Put on a brave face!'; 'Don't let them know that you are hurting.'

THE TRY HARDER PERSON

If you have found that your internal dialogue is about trying harder then you are probably always searching for something else. Just take stock of what is good about *this* job, *this* relationship. Ask yourself 'For whom am I trying harder?' You may always be looking to the future but you need to be happy in the here and now and ask for what you need now.

As a child you were well versed in 'could do better' and were often compared to brothers, sisters, cousins or others. Maybe you came home from school and said 'I came second in maths' only to be asked 'Who came first?' You were always expected to try harder. 'Do your best' is the mantra, but when you have done your best and still not received the approval of 'well done' then that's really hard.

PROFILE 2: GIVING AND RECEIVING COMPLIMENTS

It may sound simplistic, but to accept a compliment assertively all you really need to say is 'Thank you.' Assertiveness is about having the ability to respect and admit your own self-worth (receiving compliments), and that of other people (giving compliments). It is *not* about behaving in an appeasing or aggressive manner, yet is often confused with these responses (see below).

So, how did you do in assessment 2? Look back to p. 7–8 and make a note of the options you ticked below.

	A	B	C
Question 1	☐	☐	☐
Question 2	☐	☐	☐
Question 3	☐	☐	☐

QUESTION 1

Your boss compliments you on a report you have prepared. How do you respond?

For question 1 the *assertive* response is **B**, saying 'Thank you, that feels good.'

This response reflects a healthy level of self-confidence ➡ **5 POINTS**

> **ASSERTIVE BEHAVIOUR**
>
> *Assertive behaviour is about being honest, open, direct and focused. It is about asking for what you want or need, while recognizing others' needs.*

The *appeasing* response is **A**, saying 'Thanks, but I don't really think it's that great.'

This kind of response is putting yourself down and also inadvertently saying to the other person that they are not a very good judge of quality. In fact, you are discounting their compliment. It reflects unhealthy levels of self-worth and self-confidence ➡ **0 POINTS**

The *aggressive* response is **C**, thinking to yourself 'What are they after?'

This type of response is suspicious, attacking and hostile ➡ **0 POINTS**

QUESTION 2

A junior member of your team has delivered an excellent client presentation. How do you respond?

For question 2, the *assertive* response is **C**, walking over and saying 'Well done, first-rate presentation. I really think it went down well.'

This is recognizing the worth of your colleague and celebrating it. You are giving your colleague well deserved praise without undermining your own worth ➡ **5 POINTS**

The *aggressive* response is **A**, thinking to yourself 'Keep your hands off, this one's mine!'

This is demonstrating your defensiveness, possessiveness and jealousy – all aggressive attributes ➡ **0 POINTS**

> **APPEASING BEHAVIOUR**
>
> *Appeasing behaviour is about withholding your true feelings, trying to please others, feeling insecure about your relationships, role or job.*

> **AGGRESSIVE BEHAVIOUR**
>
> *When someone is aggressive they are likely to be domineering, patronizing, stubborn and hostile towards others – sometimes even violent.*

> **NON-ASSERTIVE BEHAVIOUR**
>
> *Non-assertive behaviour means behaving in either an aggressive or appeasing manner.*

The *appeasing* response is **B**, thinking 'Oh well, they'll probably want David, not me, to handle their account from now on.'

This really is putting yourself down and you are in danger of evoking a self-fulfilling prophesy of failing in the relationship. It reflects unhealthy levels of self-worth and self-confidence

➡ **0 POINTS**

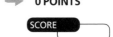

QUESTION 3

You are congratulated on winning promotion. How do you respond?

For question 3, the *assertive* response is **A**, saying 'Thanks, I'm absolutely thrilled with the promotion.'

This shows that you are able to recognize your achievements without denial or embarrassment. Well done, you have a healthy level of self-worth   ➡ **5 POINTS**

The *aggressive* response is **B**, saying 'I should think so too after all the hard work I've put into this company.'

This is a resentful reaction, demonstrating an angry and antagonistic attitude   ➡ **0 POINTS**

The *appeasing* response is **C**, saying 'It's a fluke, I don't really deserve it.'

This response shows an inability to believe in your own talent, intelligence, ability and achievement. Again, unhealthy levels of self-worth and self-confidence   ➡ **0 POINTS**

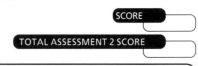

For assessment 2, the higher you score the better able you are to give and receive compliments, and the greater your self-worth and self-confidence.
Your **maximum** score is **15**.
Your **minimum** score is **0**.

PROFILE 3: BODY LANGUAGE

How you react to people's body language can depend on the amount of intimacy you have with them. If you are not direct and intimate then you will just pick up negative or positive 'vibes' and be unable to check out what you are inferring from their body language. However, if you are intimate then you will have a much better relationship with the person. You will be able to tell them what you have noticed and experienced about their body language and ask them if it relates to what they are saying.

Look back to assessment 3 (p.9) and write down your answers below.

Question 1   ....
Question 2   ....
Question 3   ....
Question 4   ....
Question 5   ....
Question 6   ....

1 Arms behind head
The most likely interpretation here is *aggressive* ('One day you'll be as intelligent as I am')   ➡ **5 POINTS**

Or *avoiding* ('I'm much too relaxed to be taking this conversation seriously')   ➡ **5 POINTS**   SCORE

2 Turned-up feet
The most likely interpretation is *adapting* ('I'm uncomfortable with what you are saying or what is being asked of me')
    ➡ **5 POINTS**   SCORE

3   Eyes lowered
The most likely interpretation here is *avoiding* (submissive because you are unable to look assertively into somebody's eyes); it can also mean feeling emotions   ➡ **5 POINTS**   SCORE

4 Pointed finger

The most likely interpretation here is *aggressive* (accusative, critical)

➡ **5 POINTS**

5 Hands on mouth

The most likely interpretation here is *adapting* (censoring, concerned at what is being said)   ➡ **5 POINTS**

6 Twirling hair

The most likely interpretation is *appeasing* (anxious, childish, nervous). Some may, mistakenly, think this is sexy

➡ **5 POINTS**

TOTAL ASSESSMENT 3 SCORE

For assessment 3, the higher you score the more adept you are at interpreting other people's body language, and the more able you are to understand and adapt your own.

Your **maximum** score is **30**.

Your **minimum** score is **0**.

So how healthy is your self-confidence? Look back to p.34 for your score for assessment 2 and write it down here   ☐

    Now your assessment 3 score   ☐

Add these individual scores together to make your **total self-confidence score:**

TOTAL SELF-CONFIDENCE SCORE

The higher your total score the more self-confident you are, and the greater your natural ability to behave assertively.
Your **maximum** score is **45**.
Your **minimum** score is **0**.

 Congratulations, you already have a healthy level of self-confidence and are skills fit. There is always room for improvement, however!

 You are moderately fit. You can be self-confident at times but there are situations that you find difficult, even intimidating. You could do with building your fitness.

 You are not skills fit! You need to do some work on building your self-confidence.

Ideally, you should work through all 10 assessments, profiles and work-outs to improve your overall fitness. However, if you have chosen to focus on developing your self-confidence ➡ Self-confidence work-out p.59. Before doing this, however, it is a good idea to do some quick mental preparation ➡ Warm-up p.54.

Getting things done

The following three profiles will help you build a picture of how assertive you are when it comes to getting things done.

PROFILE 4: MEETINGS

Look back to p.10 to remind yourself of the situations in assessment 4 and how you responded. Now make a note of the options you ticked overleaf.

	A	B	C
Question 1	☐	☐	☐
Question 2	☐	☐	☐
Question 3	☐	☐	☐
Question 4	☐	☐	☐
Question 5	☐	☐	☐
Question 6	☐	☐	☐

QUESTION 1

Someone arrives late for a meeting you are chairing; how do you respond?

For question 1 the *assertive* response is **C**, saying 'I would appreciate you coming on time to these meetings.' This is honest and direct, and doesn't resort to manipulation

 5 POINTS

 SCORE

QUESTION 2

Someone is dominating discussions. What do you do or say?

For question 2 the *assertive* response is **C**, saying 'I think it would be useful if you gave someone else the chance to air their opinions' **5 POINTS**

SCORE

QUESTION 3

Someone is wandering off the issue being discussed, in an amusing way. How do you respond?

For question 3 the *assertive* response is **A**, saying 'That's really funny, however, we do need to get through this agenda by noon. Maybe you could tell these stories over lunch?'

➡ **5 POINTS**

 SCORE

QUESTION 4

Someone keeps interrupting in the meeting; how do you respond?

For question 4 the *assertive* response is to say 'Please allow people to finish their point before interrupting' (**B**)

 **5 POINTS**

SCORE

QUESTION 5

Something is being discussed that you don't understand. How do you respond?

For question 5 the *assertive* response is **B**, saying 'I don't understand what you are saying, please will you briefly explain it to me?' **5 POINTS**

SCORE

QUESTION 6

Something is being discussed with which you do not agree; what do you say or do?

For question 6 the *assertive* response is **C**, saying 'I agree with part of what you are saying, however, I need to say that I disagree with your last point'

 **5 POINTS**

SCORE

TOTAL ASSESSMENT 4 SCORE

For assessment 4 your **maximum score** is **30**, your **minimum score** is **0**. For this assessment the higher you score the better able you are to behave assertively in meetings.

PROFILE 5: SAYING NO

Look back to p.13 in Fitness Assessment and write down your score for assessment 5 here

SCORE

For assessment 5, the higher you score the more able you are to say No to people and requests, and the more able you are to say you don't agree with a particular point of view.

Your **maximum** score is **36**.

Your **minimum** score is **−18**.

PROFILE 6: DEALING WITH MANIPULATION

Do you feel that the only way you can succeed in life is by manipulating and dominating people? Of course you don't! However, looking back to p.14 in Fitness Assessment, have you ever found yourself using some of the approaches described in the assessment? Were you able to identify the different kinds of manipulation?

MANIPULATION

People will try to manipulate you by working on certain perceived weaknesses. They may try to:

A Work on your vulnerabilities or 'crumple button'
B Appeal to your emotions
C Appeal to your intellect
D Hook your ancestral voices
E Play on your friendship
F Use their status
G Appeal to your values
H Play on your loyalty
I Make you look foolish or put you down
J Get what they want regardless of your needs.

Look back to p.14–15 and remind yourself of your responses.
Write these responses (A-J) below.

Question 1 ☐
Question 2 ☐
Question 3 ☐
Question 4 ☐
Question 5 ☐
Question 6 ☐

How did you do?

QUESTION 1
'I realize that you're keen to get away for the weekend, but
could you just do this photocopying for me before you leave?'

The preferred answer for question 1 is **B**. This comment is
playing on your emotions ⟹ **3 POINTS**

QUESTION 2
'You are the best public speaker we have, so I want you,
rather than me, to give this presentation to the staff.'

The preferred answer for question 2 is **C**. This comment is
appealing to your intellect ⟹ **3 POINTS**

QUESTION 3
'I recognize that you have to go to a funeral, however, you
must be back by 4pm for this vital meeting.'

The preferred answer for question 3 is **J**. This comment means
the other person is getting what they want regardless of
your needs ⟹ **3 POINTS**

QUESTION 4

'I know how loyal you are to me as your boss so you have to attend the residential conference regardless of the difficulties you are having with your partner.'

The preferred answer for question 4 is **H.** This comment is playing on your loyalty ➡ **3 POINTS**

QUESTION 5

LEEDS METROPOLITAN UNIVERSITY LIBRARY

'I understand how disappointed you were when you didn't get the last promotion, but this will give you the opportunity to show how the wrong person was promoted.'

The preferred answer for question 5 is **A.** This comment is working on your vulnerabilities or 'crumple button' ➡ **3 POINTS**

QUESTION 6

'I expect you to refer all queries and ideas to me as your line manager before discussing them at the directors' meeting.'

The preferred answer for question 6 is **F.** This comment is playing on status ➡ **3 POINTS**

SCORE

TOTAL ASSESSMENT 6 SCORE

For assessment 6 the higher you score the more able you are to listen to the 'music behind the words' and recognize when you are being manipulated.
Your **maximum** score is **18**.
Your **minimum** score is **0**.

So how healthy is your ability to get things done? Look back to p.39 for your score for assessment 4 and write it down here ☐
Now your assessment 5 score ☐
Your assessment 6 score is ☐

Add these individual scores together to make your **total getting things done score:**

TOTAL GETTING THINGS DONE SCORE

The higher your total score the more able you are to get things done, and the greater your natural ability to behave assertively.
Your **maximum** score is **84**.
Your **minimum** score is **–18**.

 51-84   Well done, you are already extremely fit at getting things done. Maybe there are other skills areas that you may choose to develop.

 17-50   You are moderately fit. You can get things done at times but there are situations or people that you find difficult to handle. You could do with building your fitness.

 -18-16   You are not skills fit! You need to do some work on building your ability to get things done.

Ideally, you should work through all 10 assessments, profiles and work-outs to develop overall fitness. However, if you have chosen to focus on developing your ability to get things done ➡ Getting things done work-out p.67. Before doing this, however, you really should do some quick mental preparation ➡ Warm-up p.54.

Managing conflict

The following two profiles will help you assess how assertive you are at managing conflict. Becoming more assertive will help you handle conflict, and minimize the risk of resorting to the primitive fight, flight, fright or freeze impulse.

PROFILE 7: IDENTIFYING AND MANAGING CONFLICT

So how did you do in assessment 7? Look back to p.16–18 and make a note of the options you ticked below (A-E).

Question 1   ☐
Question 2   ☐
Question 3   ☐
Question 4   ☐
Question 5   ☐

QUESTION 1
You are experiencing personal, family or relationship problems and need to take some time off work (*Inner conflict*). How do you react?

For question 1 the preferred answer is **E** – discuss with your line manager that you are having some personal difficulties and that it may be necessary to have some time away from work, which you will make up   ➡ **5 POINTS**

QUESTION 2
You are receiving complaints from several members of your staff about the slackness of one of the team (*Team conflict*). What do you do or say?

For this question the preferred answer is **E** – call the team together and ask them to voice their concerns about the 'team dynamics'   ➡ **5 POINTS**

QUESTION 3

You have to make five redundancies (*Organizational conflict*). How do you respond?

For question 3 the preferred answer is **D** – talk to all staff about the redundancies. Ask for volunteers first and then draw up a 'possibles' list, following consultation with staff and in the light of company regulations **5 POINTS**

SCORE

QUESTION 4

Two of your staff have conflict between them. They each come separately to you and complain about the other (*Conflict between two people for whom you have responsibility*). How do you deal with the problem?

A is the preferred response for this question: bringing the two members of staff together and asking them to tell each other what the issues are, and how they can be resolved
 **5 POINTS**

SCORE

QUESTION 5

You are experiencing unjust treatment, bullying or harassment from someone at work (*Conflict with one other person*). How do you respond?

The preferred answer for this question is **B** – talk to them about the behaviour that you have observed, tell them how you feel and say what you need, in terms of their treatment of you **5 POINTS**

TOTAL ASSESSMENT 7 SCORE

For assessment 7 the higher you score the better able you are to manage conflict assertively.
Your **maximum** score is **25**.
Your **minimum** score is **0.**

PROFILE 8: GIVING AND RECEIVING CRITICISM

Look back to p.19–20 in Fitness Assessment and remind yourself of the options you circled. Give yourself 3 points if you circled the options marked * below.

QUESTION 1
For the first time in months you are late for a one-to-one. Your colleague exclaims 'You are always late for my meetings!' This is invalid (unjustified) criticism. How do you respond?

A	Walk away and get angry.	1	2	3
B	Justify your behaviour.	1	2	3
C	Ask for specific examples.	1	2	3*

SCORE

QUESTION 2
You are being reprimanded in front of your colleagues (public criticism). How do you respond?

A	Say 'I think it is inappropriate to discuss this with other people present.'	1	2	3*
B	Cry.	1	2	3
C	Blame other colleagues or circumstances.	1	2	3

SCORE

QUESTION 3
Your manager has recently cancelled two meetings with you at short notice. You are annoyed and complain to a director. Your manager is then upset to receive feedback from a director rather than you first; she questions your behaviour. This is valid (justified) criticism. How do you react?

A	Say 'Well, you are never here.'	1	2	3
B	Say 'I'm sorry, you are right. It won't happen again.'	1	2	3*
C	Say nothing, and then moan to your colleagues about what a rotten manager he or she is.	1	2	3

SCORE

QUESTION 4

Some of your colleagues are feeling demotivated; you need to pass on some critical feedback to your manager. What do you say?

A 'Two members of the team are feeling very demotivated, mainly because you hardly ever praise them for the extra work they do for you in their own time.'

	1	2	3*

B 'Everyone in the team is demotivated.'

	1	2	3

C 'Everyone thinks that you are a useless manager.'

	1	2	3

SCORE

TOTAL ASSESSMENT 8 SCORE

For assessment 8 the higher you score the better able you are both to give and receive criticism. Your **maximum** score is **12**. Your **minimum** score is **0**.

So how fit are you at managing conflict? Look back to p.45 for your score for assessment 7 and write it down here ☐

Now your assessment 8 score ☐

Add these individual scores together to make your **total managing conflict score:**

TOTAL MANAGING CONFLICT SCORE

The higher your total score the more able you are to identify and manage conflict, and the greater your natural ability to behave assertively.

Your **maximum** score is **37**.

Your **minimum** score is **0**.

Well done, you are already pretty fit at identifying and managing conflict. Look for specific areas that you find more difficult.

You are moderately fit. You can manage conflict quite assertively, in most situations. You could do with building your fitness.

You are not skills fit! You need to do some work on building your ability to identify and manage conflict.

Ideally, you should work through all 10 assessments, profiles and work-outs to develop overall fitness. However, if you have chosen to focus on your ability to manage conflict ➡ Managing conflict work-out p.73. Before doing this, though, it is wise to do some quick mental preparation ➡ Warm-up p.54.

Values and rights

The following two profiles will help you understand how fit you are at asserting your values and rights.

PROFILE 9: ESTABLISHING YOUR VALUES

Look back to p.21-22 in Fitness Assessment and remind yourself of the situations and your responses (A–D). Now write these responses below.

Question 1   ☐
Question 2   ☐
Question 3   ☐
Question 4   ☐

How did you do?

QUESTION 1

You are on a selection panel for a new post. One of the candidates is black (*race*). This person is your first choice. In the post-interview discussions you hear general disquiet about his race. Telephone checks are made until some incident or reason is found to justify his non appointment.

For question 1 the preferred answer is **A** – say something immediately about what you are picking up as prejudicial comments ➡ **5 POINTS**

If you chose **D** – comment on the fact that not every candidate was checked in this way and that if a search were made on anyone some negative comment was bound to surface
➡ **3 POINTS**

QUESTION 2

A senior colleague is talking to you about a homosexual that you both know and work with (*sexuality*). Your colleague remarks 'I don't mind what they do in private, but kissing in public is disgusting. I'd give them what for if they approached me!'

For question 2 the preferred answer is **A** – ask if they object to heterosexuals kissing in public ➡ **5 POINTS**

QUESTION 3

You (a woman) are being informally interviewed for a job. You are casually asked a question about your plans for having a family (*sex/gender*).

For this question the preferred answer is **B** – say 'Have you asked all of the candidates the same question?'
➡ **5 POINTS**

If you chose **A** (respond by saying 'That seems like a sexist comment to me!') ➡ **3 POINTS**

QUESTION 4

You are invited to a mixed religion wedding. One of the guests comments on how the marriage is doomed to fail because the couple are from different religions and cultures (*religion*).

For question 4 the preferred response is **C** – say that you disagree ➡ **5 POINTS**

SCORE

If you selected **D**, say 'I believe that it is the way each person treats one another as an emotional human being that makes or breaks a marriage. It is not automatically about their religious beliefs' ➡ **3 POINTS**

SCORE

TOTAL ASSESSMENT 9 SCORE

For assessment 9 the higher you score the more able you are to establish and assert your values.
Your **maximum** score is **20**.
Your **minimum** score is **0**.

PROFILE 10: RIGHTS

Look back to p.23 in Fitness Assessment and write down your total number of ticks here ☐
For each tick ➡ **3 POINTS**

TOTAL ASSESSMENT 10 SCORE

For assessment 10 the higher you score the more able you are to assert your rights.
Your **maximum** score is **54**. Your **minimum** score is **0**.

So how healthy are you at asserting your values and rights?
Look back to p.50 for your score for assessment 9 and write it down here   ☐
Now your assessment 10 score   ☐

Add these individual scores together to make your **total values and rights score:**

TOTAL VALUES AND RIGHTS SCORE

The higher you score the more able you are to assert your values and rights, and the greater your natural ability to behave assertively.
Your **maximum** score is **74**.
Your **minimum** score is **0**.

51-74   Congratulations, you are fit at asserting your values and rights. There is always room for improvement, however!

26-50   You are moderately fit. You can assert your values and rights at times but there are situations you find difficult. You could do with building your fitness.

0-25   You are not skills fit. You need to do some work on building your ability to assert your values and rights.

Ideally, you should now have worked through all 10 assessments and profiles. If so, turn the page to discover your **overall assertiveness fitness level**.

If, however, you have focused on developing your understanding of values and rights ➡ Values and rights work-out p.78. Before doing this, however, you need to do some quick mental preparation ➡ Warm-up p.54.

How assertive are you?

You should now have completed all 10 assessments and profiles, and have a good idea of how fit you are in assertiveness.

PERSONAL FITNESS PROFILE

Look back at how you scored in the four sections:
Self-confidence
Getting things done
Managing conflict, and
Values and rights.

Make a note of your individual total scores for these sections below:

Self-confidence	☐
Getting things done	☐
Managing conflict	☐
Values and rights	☐

What is your total assertiveness score?

TOTAL ASSERTIVENESS SCORE

 155-240 Congratulations, you have a healthy level of assertiveness and are skills fit. Are there any areas you could improve still further?

 69-154 You are moderately fit. You could do with building your fitness.

 -18-68 You are not skills fit! You need to do some work and build your assertiveness.

Now take another look at your individual total scores for the four sections. Circle these scores below.

	UNFIT	REASONABLY FIT	FIT
Self-confidence	0-15	16-30	31-45
Getting things done	−18-16	17-50	51-84
Managing conflict	0-13	14-25	26-37
Values and rights	0-25	26-50	51-74

Are you strong or weak in any particular section/skills area? Are you, for example, assertive when it comes to getting things done but non-assertive when trying to manage conflict? Or perhaps you have strengths and weaknesses across all sections? Look back to your individual scores in profiles 2-10. Can you identify any particular strengths or weaknesses?

THOSE SITUATIONS IN WHICH I HAD
THE HIGHEST SCORES (STRENGTHS)

THOSE SITUATIONS IN WHICH I HAD
THE LOWEST SCORES (WEAKNESSES)

Congratulations on your strengths, but you do need to take action to develop your weaker areas. Before moving on to Work-out, you need to do some quick mental preparation  Warm-up p.54 overleaf.

Warm-up

It is wise to do a quick mental warm-up before tackling the exercises in Work-out.

Take a few moments now to reflect on your reasons for wanting to become more assertive, identifying any benefits it will bring you and others. Now think about what it might be like to be more assertive. Imagine a particular situation where you are behaving assertively...

What do you look like?
My eye contact is ....
My body posture is ....
My hands are ....

What do you sound like/what are you saying?
The tone of my voice is ....
I am saying ....

How are others reacting [positively] to you?
Others are saying ....
Others are being ....

How are you feeling?
I am feeling ....

You are now ready to make this a reality. If you have completed all 10 assessments and profiles ➡ Work-out p.55. If, however, you have chosen to focus on a particular skills area/section

➡   Self-confidence work-out p.59
➡   Getting things done work-out p.67
➡   Managing conflict work-out p.73
➡   Values and rights work-out p.78

Work-out

So, you've had your Fitness Assessment and identified your strengths and areas on which you need to work. Now is the time to take action!

Packed with practical exercises and activities, Work-out contains all the equipment you need to become super-fit at assertiveness.

Look back at your personal fitness profile on p.52-53. Where do your strengths and weaknesses lie? Do they lie in specific areas of the skill – are you, for example, generally strong when it comes to getting things done but weak when it comes to managing conflict? Or do they relate to all four skills areas? Depending on your personal fitness profile, you can either focus on improving a particular area of skill or work on individual weaknesses within each area.

Of course, if you want to raise your level of performance in all areas complete all the activities, then you really will be super-fit!

Work-outs 1-3 relate directly to profiles 1-3. Similarly, work-outs 4-6, 7-8 and 9-10.

Self-confidence

Self-confidence and a feeling of self-worth are the cornerstones of assertive behaviour. To build up your self-confidence you need to think, feel and act positively. The following three work-outs will help you achieve this.

WORK-OUT 1: ANCESTRAL VOICES

So you have discovered that those little 'creatures' that sit on your shoulder can create non-assertive behaviour. You need to become aware of these creatures and get rid of them in order to feel fit. These creatures are also sometimes referred to as *psychological drivers.*

To be physically fit, you need to start from within – eating the correct foods, digesting and excreting your rubbish. So, it is the same with your self-confidence – taking in the correct thoughts, digesting or internalizing them and eliminating any rubbish.

What follows are some positive ways of thinking; try to internalize them, think about them and accept those that are applicable to you. You may have been subjected to a great deal of rubbish over your lifetime but that does not mean you still have to carry it about with you.

The Be Perfect Person

You have a strong feeling of guilt; you are anxious about making a total mess of things. You sometimes experience feelings of worthlessness and depression.

You need to give yourself permission to appreciate the wonderful variety of human attributes and values.

The Pleasing People Person

You have a fear of being misunderstood. You constantly consider other people's needs and fear being rude to them.

You need permission to please yourself and let others

please themselves. Be free to like or dislike people. When people reject you, you don't have to reject yourself.

The Hurry Up Person

You often have a major feeling of panic, not being able to think and fatigue. You may experience a constant feeling of lateness and always hurrying to fit in too many things. You sometimes have a sense of not belonging.

You need to give yourself some selfish time.

The Be Strong Person

You often fear being unappreciated and want to stay invulnerable to others. You are easily bored.

You can't get close to people and have a sense of being unlovable.

You need to share your feelings and ask for help.

The Try Harder Person

You have a fear of failure and may think 'I could be the greatest if I could be bothered' or 'I'm not as good as I think I am.'

You need to give yourself permission to fail – and to succeed – so that you can get on with things and feel successful.

SELF-ASSERTION STATEMENTS

Self-assertion statements help establish new beliefs about yourself, and counter old ones. To do this:

1   Identify an area of your life in which you would like to be more assertive, eg speaking out in meetings.
2   Write a self-assertion statement (see below for how).
3   Read it out loud to yourself at least twice today.

Write positively, using 'I' statements and the present tense:

'I speak out clearly and confidently at meetings', *not* 'Speaking out in meetings terrifies me.'

'I respect myself for my opinions and values. I am keen to put forward my ideas to others' *not* 'No one will listen to my point of view; I am *not* valued in the organization.'

Write down below an area of your life in which you would like to be more assertive

....

....

....

Now write down a self-assertion statement

....

....

....

Read the statement out loud to yourself, visualizing real-life situations where you could put the theory into practice. Imagine the tone of voice you would use; think about how you would feel, and how others might react.

TRAINER'S WARNING

Remember, people can't read your mind. Only you can tell them how you are feeling, so do it!

Be assertive about your worth. Look after yourself, emotionally, physically and mentally. Take selfish time and enjoy it, treat yourself to small luxuries and rebuild your self-esteem.

Express your feelings and avoid turning them inward. In-turned anger can lead to depression. Say '*I* feel hurt when you treat me in that way' *not* '*You* make me feel hurt', as that gives your power away to the other person.

LANGUAGE

Using different words and language can make a tremendous difference to how you are perceived, and how you feel about yourself. Develop a strategy to improve your self-worth by changing sentences beginning with:

Should into *could*
Must into *might*
Have to into *choose to*
Ought to into *prefer to.*

This language gives you more choices, improves your sense of control and lessens any sense of guilt. We can use words like 'should', 'must', 'have to' and 'ought to' as a stick to beat ourselves with, denying ourselves choices of action.

Use assertive language – 'I wish to say'; 'I believe'; 'I think' and 'feel'; 'I need to listen' *not* 'Can I just say?'; 'Can I add to what you've just said?' This rings of permission, sounding like 'Can I just have a little breath of your air?'

The language people use can directly affect how you react to that person. Many people object to swearing or defamatory comments about work or home, but often it is more subtle. Speech might include certain words that create a feeling of unease. For example, words like:

Working '*for*' people instead of working '*with*' them
Battle language like '*axing*' the expenditure instead of '*reducing*'
'*Confronting*' or '*tackling*' people instead of '*addressing*'
'*Problems*' instead of '*issues*' or '*concerns*'
'*Why*' instead of '*what*' or '*how*'.

What words affect you and create negative feelings? Think about how you could make your responses more assertive through language.

WORK-OUT 2: GIVING AND RECEIVING COMPLIMENTS

You will get much more out of life if you are able to give and receive compliments. Learn to enjoy, not shrink from, praise. Congratulate people rather than criticize them.

TRAINER'S WARNING

Be aware of your own background. If you were brought up in a critical environment, where praise was scarce, you may unconsciously be repeating these behaviours.

Look back to profile 2 on p.32-34 to remind yourself of how you can both give, and receive, compliments assertively. Now look at the following scenarios. Think first how you want to respond – that is your *immediate* response. Is your response assertive? If so, write it down below. If not, think about what you need to say to be assertive and then write that down.

1 A colleague says 'You look good.' You say?

....
....

2 A director says 'I heard that you did a super project and that it was accepted by the client, well done.' You say?

....
....

3 A colleague has just secured a major contract with a firm you have been working on for months. What do you say?

....
....

WORK-OUT 3: BODY LANGUAGE

It is important to give positive rather than negative messages to people if you want to be perceived as being assertive. Beware of giving out unconscious, conflicting messages. For example, saying something complimentary to someone but pointing your finger at the same time may be perceived as aggressive or critical.

In order to be assertive you need to be aware of how the different parts of your body can 'talk' to other people; and how you can present a congruent, assertive image. Profile 3 on p.35 gave some pointers as to what different body language might be 'saying'. Here we explore body language, and its implications, further.

Profile 3 on p.35

> **BODY LANGUAGE**
>
> *Remember, in most face-to-face communication content accounts for 7%, voice 38% and body language 55% of someone's impression. This is why paying attention to what you do rather than what you say is so effective in looking assertive.*

Remember, there are cultural differences around the world. Some of the gestures referred to are multi-cultural, others may just belong to the Western world. For example, people of different nationalities may have different personal spaces. Some people will naturally move very close to the person to whom they are speaking (eg in the UK), whereas others might regard this as unacceptable behaviour. As might showing the under sole of your shoe or looking into the eyes of someone older or wiser than yourself. Within the same culture there will also be some people who have different preferences for body gestures; some individuals will like to be touched, others will shy away from physical contact of any kind.

BODY TALK

Ask a friend or colleague to sit down with you in a quiet room and have a 10-minute, two-way conversation about a specific issue. Imagine the meeting is quite formal; shake hands when you enter the room. Now think about how your body 'talked' during this conversation.

HEAD AND FACE TALK

How did you hold your head? How did you use your eyes and mouth? Ask your friend what they think.

To be assertive you need to:
- ✔ Hold your head at the same angle as the person to whom you are speaking.
- ✔ Look straight at a speaker when listening.
- ✔ Smile only when you are genuinely pleased.

What can you do with your head and face to look assertive?

ARM AND SHOULDER TALK

Now think about how you used your arms and shoulders. Lifted shoulders can mean 'I don't know what you're talking about.' Arms folded can mean 'I'm uncomfortable' or 'I don't want to be here.' How did you use your arms and shoulders? To look assertive, try and keep your shoulders relaxed and your arms below your shoulders.

HAND TALK

How did you use your hands? First your handshake. An aggressive, dominant handshake is one where the palm is lowered over and on top of the other person's. To shake hands assertively take your hand as far up to the other person's thumb as you can. Shake firmly; there is nothing worse than a wet fish! Equally, don't shake hands with a vice-like grip. What sort of handshake did you have? Can you develop a more assertive handshake?

How else did you use your hands? Open, relaxed hands show acceptance. 'Steepling' of hands, however, could indicate a 'know it all' or patronizing attitude.

LEG AND FEET TALK

If you cross your arms and legs you look hard to convince. Or it could indicate displeasure.

Now think about your feet. Feet can be a big give away. Remember, turned-up feet could indicate that you are uncomfortable. This gesture is called 'crying with the feet'. So, keep your feet firmly on the ground, and try not to wriggle them.

POSTURE TALK

Where you sit on the chair can indicate various things... If you lean forward then this is an invasion of the other person's space. You look as if you are ready to finish talking to them. If you sit with one arm hooked over the back of the chair this may be giving the impression 'I really don't want to be here.' How did you sit? What was your posture? To be assertive, you need to adopt an open, accepting posture. Don't invade someone else's space or give off unhelpful signals. Try and keep as still as possible; stillness is empowering.

There may be many reasons for people moving their bodies in certain ways. If you want to be assertive then a good rule of thumb is to sit in an 'open' body position while keeping as still as you possibly can; this will make the other person feel more relaxed and comfortable in your presence. Recognize that your body language may be sending out negative messages, which could be entirely opposite to those you intend. If you think this applies to you, then remember the old tip, 'Fake it till you make it!'

Self-confidence checklist

✔ Use positive language and self-assertion statements to get rid of any negative 'creatures' chatting away on your shoulder.

✔ Being assertive means recognizing your own worth, and that of other people. To accept a compliment assertively all you need to say is 'Thank you.'

> ✔ Your body language needs to be perceived as positive even though inside you may be squirming. If necessary, 'Fake it till you make it!'

Getting things done

The following three work-outs will help you develop skills of assertiveness which you can use to get things done.

WORK-OUT 4: MEETINGS

In assessment 4 we covered a range of situations which could arise in meetings – eg someone arriving late for a meeting you are chairing; someone dominating discussions, wandering off the issue or interrupting; needing to speak up when you don't agree with, or understand, something. The following tips will help you handle these, and other situations, assertively.

- ✔ Always get to meetings on time; this will encourage others to do so too.
- ✔ Speak out early, if only to say 'Good morning.' This will stop you thinking 'I'm the only one who hasn't spoken so far' and getting yourself into an anxious state. (This is the opposite behaviour of the aggressive person who loves to hear the sound of their own voice. They always voice their opinions; people often 'switch off'.)
- ✔ Keep contributions short so people keep listening.
- ✔ Avoid interrupting others and don't let others interrupt you. Say 'I would like to finish my point.' Remember, if you've been invited to join a meeting you have an equal right to be heard, seen and respected.
- ✔ Keep body language assertive – sit upright, don't slouch; stay open; make eye contact and do not fold your arms and legs simultaneously or point at people.
- ✔ Get a reaction to your contributions, as you need feedback on how your interjection has been received.

✔ Say 'Please be brief', 'Make a statement' or 'What is the point you are making?' Avoid saying 'With respect' or 'Can I just say?'; say instead 'I wish to say' or 'I think/feel that…'

✔ Make at least one positive contribution, even if it is just agreeing. This is *active* rather than passive agreement. Otherwise you will sit there thinking that everybody is involved and positive except yourself.

✔ Speaking up is easy if you believe that you are of worth. So realize that you are as OK as everyone else present. You will gain more credibility with others for speaking up (even if they disagree with what you are saying) than if you just sit there silently.

✔ Ask for clarification if anything seems unclear. It is a sign that you are listening to the arguments and still engaged in the debate. Assertive people say 'I don't understand.' By being brave enough to say what you are thinking others will probably warm towards you, and may well agree with you.

✔ Express your feelings, even though other people may find your feelings difficult to handle.

✔ Don't be afraid to check out whether other people agree or disagree with what is being said.

✔ Always confirm what people think they have to go away and do.

WORK-OUT 5: SAYING NO

Saying No to a particular person (request or opinion) can be difficult, even for naturally assertive people. Perhaps you feel intimidated by the other person, or they remind you of someone you used to be afraid of. Perhaps you are trying to gain their approval or resent their success. Whatever the reason, the following tips will help you say No when you want to:

✔ Start by realizing that you are entitled to say No. With practice, you will learn to say No without feeling guilty.

✔ In order to be assertive, and be able to say No, you need to understand how to use language in a way that positively expresses what you really want. That means not saying *Yes* when you really mean No! This means not getting pulled down avenues you don't want to go, resulting in a labyrinth of irrelevant argument. You need to continue to make your point, 'No, I am unable to do that.' You can add 'sorry' if you think it appropriate but try to just say No.

✔ Demonstrate that you are hearing what the other person is saying, 'Yes, I do realize that you have personal problems at home, however, No I cannot change the agreed arrangements.'

✔ Empathize with the other person about their situation, try to see the world through their eyes. However, if you really cannot help say No again. For example, 'That sounds very difficult for you, and I understand your concerns. However, I cannot help on this occasion.'

✔ If you do feel able to respond to their position, you could offer a compromise. However, recognize your fallback position; how far you are prepared to alter your needs to accommodate the other person's wishes. This will help you avoid being pushed further back from your own targets.

Consider the following exchange.

It's 5.30pm and your boss walks into your office:

Boss: 'I know it's late but I really need this report typed up. I would have done it myself but I had to pick Sam up from school as he was unwell. I have to meet a client at 10 tomorrow morning, can you help out?'

You are due at the cinema at 6pm to meet an old friend.

You: 'Jane, I understand your position but No I cannot stay tonight as I have an arrangement I don't want to change. However, I could come in early tomorrow and sort it out for you.'

WORK-OUT 6: DEALING WITH MANIPULATION

TRAINER'S WARNING

Watch your tone of voice as well as your words. You may be using the right words, but come across as aggressive by speaking in an abrupt, clipped way.

Remember, when people use manipulation they are looking for a pay-off. People try to manipulate you by working on certain psychological triggers or perceived weaknesses. They may, for example, try to appeal to your emotions or to your intellect. They may play on your loyalties or their status. Whatever they do, the 'broken record' technique can help you handle the situation assertively.

The phrase 'broken record' means continually repeating a clear statement of your needs and wishes. You should acknowledge the other person's point of view, but then repeat your point assertively. In effect, you will sound like an old gramophone record when the needle gets stuck in the groove and keeps repeating the same phrase over and over again.

THE 'BROKEN RECORD' TECHNIQUE

The 'broken record' technique is probably the most basic skill you need to handle manipulative behaviour. By using the technique of the broken record, combined with positive body language and concise spoken language, you can stop the manipulator achieving their goal.

The following model can help you respond to manipulation assertively.

When you	(comment on other person's behaviour)
The *effect* on me is	(state concisely how their behaviour affects your life or your feelings)
I *feel*	(share your feelings)
I *need*	(ask for what you need).

It can be helpful to begin with 'I'm finding this hard to say, however…'

Fear can prevent you from responding assertively. Recognize that you have emotional rights and that, whatever your status or salary, you are equal in terms of emotions. Try to reduce competitive feelings. Decide on your goals and be true to your values. You can always try to ask the other person for their thoughts and feelings on a situation. Ask them to empathize with how you are likely to be feeling in that situation.

If the manipulator looks upset or tearful, you can say 'I'm sorry you feel upset, however, I needed to be honest with you.' If they become angry, then you may choose to say 'I think we need to discuss this at a later stage.'

Think of something that has been said to you that you now recognize as manipulative. Replay the situation in your mind, then try to respond assertively using these phrases:

When you ....
The effect on me is ....
I feel ....
I need ....

'FOGGING'

To deal with manipulative criticism, handle conflict or achieve your goals when somebody else is constantly saying why they cannot deliver your request, you need to know about a technique called 'fogging'.

When you are being manipulated 'red herrings' are often brought in as side issues. They are talked about in order to distract you, while the manipulator is trying either to hurt you, make you angry or divert you from your goals.

'Fogging' means clearing the fog away from the specific issue or concern. With fogging you just stay with the main real issue or point; all side issues are ignored, or dealt with at a later stage.

Consider the following.

TRAINER'S WARNING

You may have heard the phrase 'the truth hurts'. Sometimes manipulative comments may hurt you because there is a grain of truth in what the person is saying; be aware of this.

'I have not received your memo... Honestly, I get so annoyed because every time I send out memos or emails to my staff, you never return yours on time. Or you just choose not to reply to me at all. I am really becoming fed up with having to ask you time and time again for your response.'

Ignoring all the padding, just concentrate on the specific which is 'I have not received your memo' and respond to that.

You could usefully include a sentence which reflects your assessment of the situation. For example, 'I'm sorry, on this occasion I have overlooked the deadline date. However, it is not true that I never respond on time.'

The technique of fogging involves being able to acknowledge that there may be some truth in what is being said to you.

By using the technique of fogging you are merely trying to stop the manipulation and protect your own self-worth. You achieve this by refusing to collaborate with any games that are being played, and therefore not rewarding the other person for their behaviour. Remember, the purpose of the other person is to make you feel hurt or upset, and deflect you from your goals. But if you don't become 'hooked' or collaborate with their games they won't feel they have achieved any 'pay-off'; they will soon tire of their antics.

Think of something that has been said to you that you recognize as manipulative criticism.

Write it down and reply to the comment using fogging.

Comment ....
....
Reply using fogging ....
....
....

> # Getting things done checklist
>
> ✔ Speak out early in meetings, if only to say 'Good morning.' Make at least one positive contribution, even if it just agreeing.
> ✔ Saying No to particular people or requests will help you manage your own work better and stop you becoming a dumping ground for other people's unwanted work.
> ✔ Address manipulation openly; clear away any red herrings using 'fogging'. Use the 'broken record' technique to get your message across.

Managing conflict

You may dislike conflict, but resolving it assertively can bring positive outcomes. The following two work-outs offer you practical tips and advice for dealing assertively with conflict.

WORK-OUT 7: IDENTIFYING AND MANAGING CONFLICT

Look back to assessment and profile 7 to remind yourself of the different forms conflict can take, and how you dealt with them. Did you face the conflict openly and calmly or did you try and hide from it? There are five main ways of dealing with conflict:

Avoiding
Appeasing
Attacking
Adapting
Addressing.

Which is your preferred style? Check out the following situation. How would you respond?

A client complains to you about delays in your overly bureaucratic system. What do you do (tick the appropriate box)?

A Agree with them about the stupid rules. ☐
B Tell them they deserve to be delayed and that it's their fault. ☐
C Ask them to tell you the facts of the case and then act on the evidence presented. ☐
D Say 'It's nothing to do with me.' ☐
E Say 'Don't worry, it will turn out all right.' ☐

Which one did you choose?

Answer D - AVOIDING
Answer E - APPEASING
Answer B - ATTACKING
Answer A - ADAPTING
Answer C - ADDRESSING

People's styles depend on how important goals and relationships are to them. Ideally, you need to aim to *address* conflict to behave assertively. You need to:

✔ Separate the issue from the person.
✔ Clarify the issues; share your perceptions of the conflict and the desired outcome.
✔ Take one issue at a time and avoid using examples from the past (this can lead to distortion and manipulation since the other person is likely to have forgotten the incident or remember it differently).
✔ Be honest about your needs and feelings. Use clear 'I' statements; this takes responsibility for yourself and avoids blaming other people for how you feel.
✔ Remember, this is not about winning or losing. You need to work towards a win-win outcome *together*. Brainstorming ideas can sometimes help.

Think of a situation where you were involved in conflict (it might be simplest if you recall a situation where you were in conflict with just one other person). How did you react? Did you behave assertively? If yes, well done! If no, replay the situation in your mind, but this time try to *address* the situation; behave assertively.

WORK-OUT 8: GIVING AND RECEIVING CRITICISM

There will be times when you are criticized, so it is important that you are able to handle criticism in a way that is productive to both you and the critic.

RECEIVING CRITICISM

Think of an example when someone has criticized you:

1 What exactly did they say?

....

....

2 How did you respond?

....

....

3 What was the outcome?

....

....

Now ask yourself:

1 Was the criticism valid (justified) or invalid (unjustified)?

....

....

2 If it was valid criticism, did you agree with them?

....

....

> **TRAINER'S TIP**
>
> *You are allowed to make mistakes so admit them! Using humour, eg 'That's the first mistake I ever made!', can help diffuse tension.*

3   If it was invalid criticism, did you disagree with what the person said and say why it was invalid?

....

....

4   Was the criticism vague?

....

....

5   Did you ask them to give you specific examples of their criticism of your behaviour?

....

....

6   Who had the problem?

....

....

7   What could you do differently next time to improve the experience?

....

....

When receiving criticism some people start to justify their behaviour; others say nothing but feel angry or upset. Still others respond by blaming someone else. How do you react? First of all you will need to decide if the criticism is valid or invalid. For example, you are told:

'You never meet deadlines...'
Valid?   Yes? Then agree.
Invalid?   Yes? So say so and say why it is invalid.

However, what often happens is:

Critic: 'You never meet deadlines!'

You: 'Oh yes I do, it's just that you expect more and more of me and if I had more resources I could get the job done quicker. It's impossible trying to work to deadlines here because so many staff are either off sick or are sent to work off-site and nobody knows where they are or when they are returning. I can never get in touch with them to get the information I require to finish my report...' and so on.

You have resorted to defending and justifying your behaviour. Remember that you have the following options:

VALID	INVALID		
Agree	Say it's invalid and why	Ask for specific examples	Who's got the problem?
Apologize and explain. This takes the heat out of the situation.	Perhaps there is a misunder-standing.	Criticism needs to be focused.	Say 'I can see that is a problem for you.' This should be the last resort, try the other suggestions first.

Watch out for language that makes people feel uneasy – 'confront' or 'tackle' rather than 'address'; 'problems' rather than 'issues'; 'should' instead of 'may'. Also, watch your tone of voice and delivery – don't be abrupt.

GIVING CRITICISM

As well as receiving criticism you may sometimes have to give critical feedback to others:

- ✔ Be specific; give instances rather than being vague.
- ✔ Comment on a person's *behaviour* (which can be changed) rather than their personality (which can't).

✔ Recognize that *you* may be wrong and that the other person could have a good and valid reason for what has happened; you will not know about it unless you ask them.

✔ Recognize your prejudices and stereotyping.

Managing conflict checklist

✔ Most people deal with conflict in one of five main ways, from avoiding to attacking. Learn to *address* conflict.

✔ If you are criticized assess whether the criticism is valid or invalid. If valid acknowledge this and explain your actions. If invalid, say so and why. Ask for specific examples of behaviour.

Values and rights

The final two work-outs offer advice on how to assert your values and rights.

WORK-OUT 9: ESTABLISHING YOUR VALUES

You will always find individuals within a group who share your values (and to whom you can relate well), and some who don't. Be aware of this, and also of your own prejudices – maybe you don't like someone's appearance or accent. Maybe you resent their success. Treat everyone fairly, regardless of their values (and in spite of your prejudices). Assert your own values in both your words and deeds. Speak honestly and directly, while recognizing that others also have values.

WORK-OUT 10: RIGHTS

Now for your final work-out. Look back to p.23 in Fitness Assessment and remind yourself of the statements you didn't tick, and how you felt about them (frightened, angry, embarrassed?).

The essence of assertiveness is understanding that both you, and other people, have certain rights. You must recognize your own rights, and those of other people. If you have rights you find difficult to accept, look back over the book and learn how to assert these rights – without being perceived as aggressive. Which right/s will you try to work on now? Will you exercise any of your other rights? Remember:

- ✔ You have the right to be heard, but equally you need to listen to others.You have the right to assert yourself, and so do other people.
- ✔ You have the right to state what you want, but you also need to recognize others' needs.
- ✔ You have the right to feel, but need to realize that other people have emotions too. Treat people as emotional human beings not as roles.
- ✔ You have the right to make mistakes. Remember that 'people who never make mistakes never make anything.'
- ✔ You have the right to be protected by the law, but you also need to live within the law.
- ✔ You have the right to free speech, but remember the effect your language will have upon others if you make racist, sexist or abusive comments.
- ✔ You have the right to feel secure, but remember that security is a state of mind and comes from within. Avoid creating insecurity by stirring up fear, anxiety and destructive gossip.
- ✔ You have the right to be happy, so if you were given a joyless script as a child then give yourself permission to change it. Try saying 'It's OK to be happy'.

✔ You have the right to be ill, so stop trying to play the martyr. Look after your physical and mental health.

✔ You have the right to be treated with respect, but remember, you also need to treat others with respect.

✔ You have the right to grieve, so give yourself permission to cry, feel sad and express you feelings.

✔ You have the right to give others their rights, so learn to empower people.

✔ You have the right to enjoy your sexuality, as long as it is not in the form of harassment or impinges upon others people's boundaries.

✔ You have the right not to be overlooked, but it is up to you to make your mark and be seen.

✔ You have the right not to be emotionally abused, however, people cannot read your mind so you need to tell them when you feel this way.

✔ You have the right not to be physically abused so it is up to you to distance yourself from the perpetrator. This is easier said than done for many people, but if you work on your own feelings of self-worth and self-love then you will reach a stage of recognizing that you are no longer prepared to live or work where such behaviour exists.

Values and rights checklist

✔ Treat everyone fairly, regardless of their values, and inspite of your prejudices.

✔ Assert your own values in words and deeds.

✔ Recognize that you have rights and so do other people.

Keeping Fit

Well, congratulations on finishing the book! Hopefully you have enjoyed the experience and gained from the advice and insights offered.

As you have discovered, assertiveness is a powerful and empowering skill. But, like any skill, practice makes perfect, and the more times you use it the better you get at it. You need to keep skills fit, and this is what the final part of this book is all about...

Keeping fit

As mentioned at the very start of this book, assertiveness is a key skill for success both at work and home, and it is important that you don't let it slip.

You need to keep on your toes, keep practising. If you feel your skills slipping then look through the book again, remind yourself of the key learning points, even run through a couple of exercises. Better still, set yourself some real-life targets *now* to keep yourself up to scratch. These could be anything from volunteering to chair a meeting within the next month to initiating conversation with someone in the organization that you've never spoken to before within the next hour.

Make a note of your targets in your personal fitness plan below (bearing in mind the benefits it will bring you, or others). Specify actions and time-scales; this will keep you focused and fit.

Personal fitness plan

Target/Action	By when	√
....		
....		
....		
....		
....		
....		
....		
....		
....		
....		
....		
....		

Further Reading

Further reading

Civil, Jean, *Being Assertive*, Salix Publishing Ltd, 1997

Civil, Jean, *Coping with Conflict*, Salix Publishing Ltd, 2001

Dickson, Anne, *A Woman in Your Own Right*, Quartet, 1983

Dickson, Anne, *The Mirror Within*, Quartet, 1985

Fleming, James, *Become Assertive*, David Grant Publishing Ltd, 1997

Lindenfield, Gael, *Assert Yourself*, Thorsons, 2001

Lloyd, Sam, *How to Develop Assertiveness*, Kogan Page, 1988

O'Brien, Paddy, *Assertiveness: A Working Guide*, Nicholas Brealey Publishing

Stubbs, David, *Assertiveness at Work*, Macmillan, 1997